TO AMNTIE LINDA
LOVE CHLOE Brodkin
ChloeBrodkin

Heartfilled Poetry

By Chloe Brodkin

A Bird is Calling

1st A bird is calling from a distance, voice is so strong, I can't help but hear it.

Chorus: Spirit voice flows in you, be strong, hold on.

2nd You know it, don't deny it, hold on.

Chorus

3rd No one's going to stop you now, keep on going, you aren't going down now. If you are, I'll come with you. I'll always be here, don't go down, and then you'll be gone forever, stay strong, hold on.

Chorus: Be strong, or get out of here.

4th A bird is calling you now.

❖ **Dedicated to all the writers in the world.**

Acceptance

People obsess over personality, and gender. Why does the way you look, and act matter so much? Everyone loves to judge, we look at everything around us, and form assumptions based on what we see. If you put yourself in someone else's shoes, than you understand them better, and don't judge them. We want to be equal, but if we always judge, how can we be equal?

The times change, and the years flow fast. But humans remain sensitive, and insecure, and focus on superficial matters. How can we help everyone feel loved, and accepted?

I guess, we can't, because there isn't enough validation in the world, to go around. Most people, don't even accept themselves, how can they accept other people?

Society is superficial, we can't change that, but we can learn to be sensitive to what others think, and more importantly, how others feel. Then we won't be so selfish, and we can change the world by thinking about others, before ourselves.

A Girl's mind

Every girl hates her body. Everyone has faults they can't diminish. We are too anxious, or not spontaneous, or not gutsy enough. There's no way to make us perfect, and we'd rather not be, but it's very hard to accept ourselves, for who we are inside.

A New Way to live

1st Time runs thin, time goes slow, and time is with you, more than you know.

Chorus: It's a new start, it's a new norm, it's yours to see, and yours to control. It's a new way with your new skin; you're doing it today, you're finding a new way to live.

2nd You've been lost; now you're found, take a look around, you'll see, this is a new place to be.

Chorus

3rd You've got your life back together, controlling it, it's yours to stick to, and yours to hold.

Chorus

4th Everything around you is yours, it's there for you, because time got you through, it told you to make a new world.

Chorus

5th Here you are, here we all are, we are finding a new way to live, because we've found our new skin, it's in us, and we took the change, and we fell, and got back up again in the end.

Chorus

6th We're doing it together, because we got a new place to start.

1. Tune. Song. Bryans Adams. Here I am. Spirit Stallion Movie. 2002.

2. Book. Laurie Halse Anderson. Speak. 1999.

Ann

1st Ann, you've got a long way to go. You've got to stop cutting yourself short. Trust you're a beauty, and see, you can live any life you want to, and be whoever you want to be, and it's up to you.

Chorus: You got to stand up, take control be bold, and have no fear. You got to be happy you're here. You've got to see all the wonderful things you can be, if you let yourself dream. You don't have to be a governess, don't wait on them hand and foot, there's no sorrow for you.

2nd Go out and live your life, be the quiet character, I know you are, and never cut yourself short again.

3. Book. Libba Bray. The Gemma Doyle Trilogy. A Great and Terrible Beauty. 2006.

At the end of the day

1st You're your own worst critic, that's what they say. But you got through it, at the end of the day.

Chorus: I know you were nervous, you thought you would faint, but you got through it, at the end of the day.

2nd We're all here to help you, if you struggle in anyway. We'll always be there, day after day.

Chorus

3rd If you can do this, you can do anything, if you just believe, there are endless possibilities.

Belle "Out There"

Prologue: Disney Princess Belle with black hair, she is walking towards a library.

"I just don't see things the way he does. I don't see how a world that is, so boring, could be so useful".

"I want to be in the library". I want to see, want to see the snow. What's laughing, and how does it work?" "Married to him won't get me too far; out there I can be smart, with all those books wild and free, wish I could be out there". "Oh what would I give, if I could live out of this town?" "Out there, they would understand a love of reading". I'm sick of dreaming ready to see".

"I'm ready to know what they know out there, ask them my questions, and get some answers". "What's happiness, and how does it flow?"

"When it's my turn, and I'd love, love, to explore the world out there". "Out of this town, wish, I could be out there". "I don't know when, I don't know how, but I know something's starting right now". "Watch and you'll see, someday I'll be, out there searching for me".

4. Movie. Disney. Beauty and the Beast. Belle. 1991.

5. Tune and Lyrics. Movie. Disney. The Little Mermaid. Part of your World. 1989.

Bliss

1st People come, and people go, you don't know why they pass you by, it feels like they're giving up on you (all the time) sing twice.

Chorus: You got to find the bliss, feel that happiness, what keeps you alive is what's inside.

2nd Let the world know, that you're there, don't be scared to care, but it's meant to be, when people pass you by, don't let them see you cry.

Chorus

3rd Keep close to your bliss, make life fix you up, make bliss keep you happy, and strut your stuff.

Chorus 4th You have to find it, glide through life, like its hot water, there's no struggle, when you've found your bliss.

Blue Jay

1st He wears a mask, time marks his path. The road he is on is a dangerous one.

Chorus: You got to wait for your fate to get better, let us brighten your sun.

2nd Every road you take, everything you hold. You got to trust it can get you there, and save you from death, you've got to believe us.

Chorus

3rd Wait is all you have to do, to save you.

6. Book. Cornelia Funke. Inkheart. 2003.

Children's Promise

Chorus: You got to let them go, they can live their life, you've taught them everything they know, and now it's time to go.

1st It'll be alright, they'll never go away all together; a piece will always be left for you.

Chorus

2nd No matter what, they'll be with you, this is a children's promise, which will never fade.

Chorus

3rd They can live their own life, and carry on the message, to keep this promise alive.

Create

We are always desperate to create something. We want to fashion it our way. That is the only way we can leave something behind, and we want to be remembered for it by, and by.

7. Book. Louisa May Alcott. Little Women. 1868.

Fantasy Land

I journeyed to a faraway land on a ship. This land is filled with scary goblins, and fairies, and blood. I pricked my finger on a thorn bush, and fell into a deep sleep. I woke up bleeding, and now I know it's from the thorn bush, and the fantasy land.

I have to stop living in fantasy, and get back to reality. But I go to the fantasy land, when I'm feeling lonely. There I feel better; there I'm not depressed, there I'm understood.

Felicity

Chorus: You got to learn to trust and know you must care. Go with the flow, feel what you want to feel, but your family of friends has to stick together. You have to trust them now and forever no matter what, I swear it'll be better than your stubbornness.

1st Laugh, and play loud, but don't forget to believe they are there for you and now you shall trust them too.

Chorus

2nd We'll all be there for you, if you can care and trust with all your life, and it can be just us. Then you'll be kinder and create your life according to what you want, not what other people want or expect. Now all you have to do is care and trust your whole life through that is your reward. 8. Book. Libba Bray. The Gemma Doyle Trilogy. A Great and Terrible Beauty. 2006.

Fenoglio

1st Stuck in a book, death is controlling your story, you've lost all self-control, you've lost the power of words.

Chorus: You got to make a happy ending, turn back the book, right side up. Find the power of words again.

2nd Find yourself in your world again. To make it last, you've got to change the past.

Chorus

3rd Create your new world, and gain control once more, you've got to learn to care, be there to change it.

9. Book. Cornelia Funke. Inkheart. 2003.

Fragile

1st The whole world is talking about me, that's how it feels. I'm done with him, I've got my life on track and I'm going to show the world, so they don't say I'm bad.

Chorus: You think I'm fragile you think I'm nothing but glass, but I know I've got more class.

2nd You're a jock stepping off the street hard as rock too tough to beat, while I'm just glass to you?

Chorus

3rd You're so stubborn it's like you don't know who I am , but if you take one look at me, it looks like you're looking through me. Chorus 4th It's nothing at all, I didn't even have to fall. I just played by myself. Listen now, I know I don't want to be on your team.

Chorus

5th Making my effort was too tough; I was forced to give up. Going through school like this is the real pain, I miss my old friends it seems like they dissed me, but I know who is true and that's not you.

6th Now you won't bring me down. You have faded away and my group will stay.

Chorus

7th If you don't know me it doesn't matter to me. You can go hurt who you want to and be who you want to be. You can see it's your life and I'm seeing mine, I'm not coming back to you this time. Chorus 8th I'm going where I belong, where I feel strong and not depressed. People will test me but I'll tell them to get a life, I'm going to be myself and start living my life.

Chorus

9th Glass can be broken, but not me, I'll get strong and set myself free.

Friends (There for you)

I'll be there for you, rain or shine, risk my life, for such a great and loyal group of friends. Share time to the end. Yes, you know it is true; I'll be there for you. Until the end of time, you're my friends and I'll always be there for you.

Good and Evil

Good and evil is the name of the game. But what if good and evil got along? What if they were "Play" fighting? But then again a child's mind is not warped by revenge like an evil queen's, or a pirate's. What if the evil queen turned good, and the "Savior" turned dark? And if the "Dark one" became a hero? Then what would hell look like? What would happen if good became evil? And evil became good? Which world would you choose to live in?

10. TV Show. Once Upon a time. 2011.

Home

A child wishes for a home, others take for granted. She doesn't want to walk; it's so far back the way she came. There's a light at the end of the tunnel, I hope will lead her home soon. She only has a doll to reminder her of the home she once had.

11. Movie. Madeline. 1998.

I'm the Dreamer

1st I believe in myself now. I'm a dreamer, like every girl. I can make choices in this life. They're mine, I control everything, this is the time.

Chorus: I'm the dreamer, here to start again. Find someone better, for I'm not alone again.

2nd I'm the dreamer. If you let yourself dream for a minute, you'll be free ask me. I'm the dreamer, it's my choice.

Chorus

3th I'm the dreamer, remember life never ends, and things are beyond what you see. I'm the dreamer, living this life; it's mine to hold onto uptight. I'm living the life, which will never end. I'm the dreamer, and this is the time to believe in me, and never let it go.

Imagination

An author is trapped in her little world. We are all trapped in our imaginations, and the only way to get out is to write about what we see, think and feel in the world about us.

Ironic Change

1st In the nick of time everything can change. You don't know when it's going to change, but in the blink of an eye it's going to be so sudden.

Chorus: It's all going to change in the blink of an eye, in the nick of time; it's going to be an ironic change.

2nd In the nick of time things can change, in the blink of an eye it's going to be unexpected, already ironic, but you know mother won't have to tell me it's going to change. The changes of the past can go with the future but either way years will go by, and someday it's all going to change unexpectedly.

Chorus

3rd Even your mind can think crazy thoughts. You'll try to escape it, but it has to be done in everyone's life.

In the nick of time, or in the blink of an eye, you can change, and it can be ironic, unexpected it can change in the nick of time; in the blink of an eye, it will be ironic.

Jealousy

Jealousy is like a festering tornado, it won't stop, until it's consumed your soul. It won't stop, until you learn the lesson of gratitude, and be content with what you have. You always have what you need, and what you want will come in time, if you keep love in your life. Keep all doors open in your mind, you never know, what you will find there.

Little Women Quotes

"You have so many extraordinary gifts. How can you expect to lead an ordinary life?"

This quote was said, in a conversation between Jo and her mom. I think all readers and people who are different can relate to this quote, you will always be unique, and you should never be afraid to be yourself.

"There are many Beths in the world, shy and quiet, sitting in corners till needed and living for others so cheerfully that no one sees the sacrifices till the little cricket on the hearth stops chirping, and the sweet, sunshiny presence vanishes, leaving silence and shadow behind."

"I want to do something splendid...something heroic or wonderful that won't be forgotten after I'm dead.

I don't know what, but I'm on the watch for it and mean to astonish you all someday."

"Girls are so queer you never know what they mean. They say no when they mean yes, and drive a man out of his wits just for the fun of it".

"Let us be elegant or die!"

"I don't see how you can write and act such splendid things, Jo. You're a regular Shakespeare!" exclaimed Beth, who firmly believed that her sisters were gifted with wonderful genius in all things.

"I think we are all hopelessly flawed".

12. Book. Louisa May Alcott. Little Women. 1868.

Loss Quote

"What I was really researching was not how elephants deal with loss but how humans can't".

This quote was said, by the character Alice Metcalf in the book *Leaving time* written by Jodi Picoult. Alice Metcalf was the mom in the story and she never got over the loss of her daughter. The daughter, Jenna Metcalf felt like a part of herself was missing without her mom. This story symbolizes the importance of family and how devastating loss is.

13. Book. Jodi Picoult. Leaving time. 2014.

Memories

Memories are your life. When you love someone who dies they're with you every day.

You know they live in you, when you look in the mirror and see them staring back at you.

Your life goes on and on but your experiences and the people you love stay with you.

They are written in your mind and in your soul.

Like a princess in a castle your memories are your life.

New Day

It's a new day today. I'm going to stop missing someone who doesn't accept me for who I am. It's finished, it's done and I'm the one who won because I accept myself as I am today.

Order

1st You've got the power to let go. You've got the power to see the world if you want to. You've got the power to change it if you dare. There's something in the air.

Chorus: You're part of the order you've got the power to save the realms. Bind the magic with the temple; don't let the winterland creatures get there first. They all think you're a disaster now, but time will show them you're the master and only you can save the realms.

2nd Everybody needs you though they may not know it yet. They'll be helping you to frolic and flow in this world of the realms. The world your mother made, she is in peace now. She will be proud for her daughter has got the power within her skin to bind the magic and get rid of all the tragic things she knows.

Chorus

3rd You've got the power to save these realms before it's too late

and bind the magic. Do the task your mother never could.

14. Book. Libba Bray. The Gemma Doyle Trilogy. A Great and

Terrible Beauty. 2006.

Pack

1st We've got to move again. We're on the road again.

Chorus: Pack and repack, pack and repack, do you think we got it easier than you?

2nd It's a long way to go with a tempered mother in your life, this is well don't bother, for life is an open road to me.

Chorus

3rd Definitely life will be your own; you'll know this is the way to be.

Chorus

4th No one's life is easy, and you can't control it, so go pack.

Pippa

1st Pippa, you've got to be strong and don't get corrupted.
You've got to pass over, or else you'll suffer the darkness, you will become.

Chorus: They say they can fix you, but in the end I am sad to tell you. You have to stay in the darkness, and be corrupted, or pass onto a golden path. You must listen to me, for I've got the power in these realms; this is the only way to save you. Are you listening to me Pippa?

2nd We do care about you, but there's this air about you which says you'll be corrupted. You've got to learn to face the facts, and don't look back.

Chorus 3rd Listen to me, you've got to flee over to the other side. I'll meet you there, and it will be alright, you'll be a new Pippa, when you've been saved.

15. Book. Libba Bray. The Gemma Doyle Trilogy. A Great and Terrible Beauty. 2006.

Please us

1st It all depends on you, what you do, what you write, everything starts with the fight.

Chorus: We're all counting on you, can't you see it too? You're still the author living a story book and we want you to look inside yourself.

2nd Remember your story, feel it inside. You've got to know the happy ending from your head to your toe, and put it down on paper. This will make everyone safer.

Chorus

3rd Finish this story and then read it aloud. Believe it and live it, it's the thing to be found. If you let it flow then you'll know the feeling of letting go.

Chorus

4th You've got the book back on track, and you'll be helping it

forevermore.

16. Book. Cornelia Funke. Inkheart. 2003.

Power of Words

1st With the power of words evil can be revenged, stereotyping can be banished. The right voice can make all the evil go away and you can stay in a world that's been made for you.

Chorus: If you could make words have a power. If you could leave all the darkness behind, you should find a peaceful place. It will be a new beginning to start; you'll be the boss, with the power of words at your side. 2nd With the power of words you can do anything, with the power of words you can speak out. Have your opinion heard; stick them up to their necks in shame if that's your game.

Chorus

3rd If you want you can go away or stay for the power of words can help you solve all your problems if you only didn't run away. You could stay forever in a written world.

Chorus

4th The power of words can make you happy. With the power of words you can go off now and make a new start for you've got the power at your side and it will be your guide to your destiny. You can do anything, for the power of words, will be never ending.

Chorus 2: The power of words will be in your hands to stay and make all your problems go away. If you only believe the words are at your side, that's it's solve or be depressed, don't get stressed, use the power of words.

5th You'll make your own written world to live in. This is my written world, go find your own.

17. Book. Cornelia Funke. Inkheart. 2003.

Relax

We are always busy, never stopping and we don't know why. If we could take a step back and relax, we would all be fine.

What's happening with the world today? Why do we keep making the same mistakes? If we would only listen, if we would only learn, not to judge or criticize we wouldn't have to burn.

We are part of the human condition always doing, what we have to do. What do we want? How can we relax a bit more?

Steve Jobs Quote

"The people, who are crazy enough to think they can change the world, are the ones who do".

18. Quote. Steve Jobs.

Teachers

Chorus: Study, study, study, that's what we do. Study, study, study, that's all you want us to do.

1st It's always work; work us to the bone, hardly ever home.

Chorus

2nd Test after test you work us till we're fried. Assignment after assignment, you have us cooking now.

Chorus

3rd I know it stands for good intentions. Don't wait, give us a break, we're students waiting for summer.

Chorus

4th More tests more than I have sleepovers, so please have some sense, don't digress, and give us a break.

Chorus 5th That's all you teachers do to help us.

The Light

The light is tired of peaking in through the dark. It has to give up and sink into the shadows. This is why people can't think in the shadows because they can't see the light. To them it doesn't exist and they are drowning in the shadows. The light has given up and there is nothing left, but shadows and darkness that will turn even the best intentions to stone.

We could all just give up but we don't even when our hearts have turned dark. Then we live for revenge and vengeance of the people who have wronged us but we are never satisfied with that either. There is no rest for the wicked so it's easier to be good even if we are struggling within ourselves to find the little seed of good and plant it again. If we plant it, everything will be alright, when it starts to grow.

Someday we will find the magic bean, and journey to a new land, and start anew. We can find where we belong, where there are people, who are just beginning to see the light, just like us.

19. TV Show. Once Upon a time. 2011.

The Nursery

The nursery simulates whatever you can think about. If you want to go somewhere, it will take you there. It's a great alternative to getting a nanny or a baby sitter. The nursery is great for so many reasons. It can make you forget about life's problems, by taking you to your happy place.

The nursery can also help you raise your children. If you want them to go on an educational trip the nursery can make that happen.

It is also great if your significant other is mad at you for some reason. You can think of a happy room for you to stay in away from him.

This nursery has some ware and tare. It has some minor glitches but those can be fixed easily enough. It had a minor accident with the previous owner. That issue is solved now.

The nursery was used a fair amount but that does not affect how it works or the great value of it. Simply imagine your happy place and go to it when you are feeling trapped in a devastating situation. The nursery will never lose its value; it's too good for that.

 The nursery will remain always for children and anyone who needs a happy place to escape from reality. The nursery is your imagination and your playground forever.

20. Movie. Disney. Marry Poppins. 1964.

The Runaway Bride

She has to hide, she has a broken heart, everyone has the rotten start. When love gets sour it gives you the power to move on. She sings her song, and goes through her life barely breathing, for she knows what it's like to see everything at once. There's always hope. It keeps her going, hope there is something better and something more than this life. Hope is her light at the end of the tunnel. The runaway bride has to find her happy place in the sky. There she can be alone and free, content up there, she will stay, until we find her one day.

Throw the candle out

1st It is the end, but it's okay. We'll find something better someday.

Chorus: Throw the candle out, looks like I'm solo tonight, but I know I'll be alright.

2nd Someday it'll be new again, and we won't look back this time.

Chorus:

3rd I'm sorry, but we have to throw the candle out, and stop

trying this time. I know I'll be alright.

21. TV Show. Glee. 2009.

Train

Life is like a speeding bullet train. Sometimes you desperately

want to get off it. You feel like beating down the door and

thrashing around. But you can't get off it and you never will.

Time never stands still. And that's okay, its life, and you freak

out sometimes. When your emotions are heightened or you are

stressed out and mad at the world, so mad you want to take a

vase and throw it at someone, so it shatters into a million pieces,

sliding across the floor.

Wicked

1st No one mourns the wicked, how can this be so?

Chorus: We are all the same inside. All we want is to be

accepted and belong somewhere.

2nd People have to agree to disagree, for they can't change. And

they won't change ever.

Chorus

3rd Are we all good? Can we change for good? Or will the bad

always be bad?

22. Musical. Stephen Schwartz. Winnie Holzman. Wicked.2003.

You're not a piece of me

1st It doesn't matter to you, it doesn't matter to me. I have to make the world see.

Chorus: You're not a piece of me; I'm not a broken heart. I think I found the perfect place to start.

2nd I don't need you to be there every step of the way, hearts are broken every day. I can deal with this; this is me without you. I don't need to doubt myself anymore; it's over now you don't have to care anymore.

Chorus

3rd I don't need all the drama, it's left behind in last year, it's not going to be here.

Chorus 4th I got my true friends they're loyal to me now. I've got to make the world see and you.

Chorus 5th I'm deleting you out of my life because you're not a piece of me. The world can see the real me because you're not a piece of me. Get out of my life; everything will be alright because you're no longer a piece of my heart.

Heartfilled Poetry Manuscript References List

1. Tune. Song. Bryans Adams. Here I am. Spirit Stallion Movie. 2002.

2. Book. Laurie Halse Anderson. Speak. 1999.

3. Book. Libba Bray. The Gemma Doyle Trilogy. A Great and Terrible Beauty. 2006.

4. Movie. Disney. Beauty and the Beast. Belle. 1991.

5. Tune and Lyrics. Movie. Disney. The Little Mermaid. Part of your World. 1989.

6. Book. Cornelia Funke. Inkheart. 2003.

7. Book. Louisa May Alcott. Little Women. 1868.

8. Book. Libba Bray. The Gemma Doyle Trilogy. A Great and Terrible Beauty. 2006.

9. Book. Cornelia Funke. Inkheart. 2003.

10.   TV Show. Once Upon a time. 2011.

11.   Movie. Madeline. 1998.

12.   Book. Louisa May Alcott. Little Women. 1868.

13.   Book. Jodi Picoult. Leaving time. 2014.

14.   Book. Libba Bray. The Gemma Doyle Trilogy. A Great and Terrible Beauty. 2006.

15.   Book. Libba Bray. The Gemma Doyle Trilogy. A Great and Terrible Beauty. 2006.

16.   Book. Cornelia Funke. Inkheart. 2003.

17.   Book. Cornelia Funke. Inkheart. 2003.

18.   Quote. Steve Jobs.

19.   TV Show. Once Upon a time. 2011.

20.   Movie. Disney. Marry Poppins. 1964.

21.   TV Show. Glee. 2009.

22.   Musical. Stephen Schwartz. Winnie Holzman. Wicked. 2003.